TOBY'S FABLE: THE BUREAUCRACY & THE FARMER

FELTON WILLIAMSON, Jr.

W9-CBE-523

Revised: 2/22/2014

ISBN-13:
978-1494999117

ISBN-10:
1494999110

<u>FOREWORD</u>

"A Toby's Fable" is a fictional account of the Aristocracy's use of the Bureaucracy to increase the profits of their cronies. The action drives small farmers out of business, limits consumer's choices and increases egg prices. While this is a fictional story, similar oppression is all too common in our society. Are you at risk? When was the last time you saw an "EGGS FOR SALE" sign on a farmer's lawn?

"A Toby's fable" is more like a long, fully illustrated (16 cartoons) magazine article than a book. But you won't find a better description of the creeping tyranny that is destroying America.

Table of Contents

TOBY'S FABLE: EGGS INCORPORATED AND THE BUREAUCRACY

Once upon a time there was a proud, prosperous farmer who earned a good living growing corn, raising chickens and marketing "free range chicken eggs".

The farmer used "free range" chickens to produce the eggs because "free range" chicken eggs commanded a higher price. Even though it took more labor and space to take care of the "free range" chickens, the higher price more than paid for the extra cost of the eggs. Besides, the farmer and his customers knew that his eggs tasted better and were more nutritious than those mass produced eggs marketed by EGGS INCORPORATED.

All was well. The farmer was making a good living providing a quality product and consumers enjoyed a quality product.

"Free range" chickens forage for food but the major portion of the chickens' diet was provided by the farmer's corn crop so the farmer's expense in producing such a quality product was extremely limited. The farm was very profitable. The farmer and his family were happy even though many hours of labor were required to grow the corn, care for the large flock of happy "free range "chickens and market the eggs.

"FREE RANGE" CHICKENS FORAGE FOR FOOD

THE "FREE RANGE" WELL CARED FOR CHICKENS PRODUCE DELICIOUS, NUTRITIOUS EGGS

FARMER'S HAPPY CHILDREN ENJOY FEEDING CORN TO THE "FREE RANGE" CHICKENS

TOTALLY UNAWARE THEY WILL SOON BE VICTIMS OF THE BUREAUCRACY!

THE EGGS INCORPORATED BOARD OF DIRECTORS MEETS:

Meanwhile, the Board of Directors of EGGS INCORPORATED met to discuss the destructive competition from private farmers producing eggs for the local markets. The board was especially concerned about farmers using gimmicks like "free range" chickens to give their product an unfair advantage over EGGS INCORPORATED products. Besides, unregulated egg farmers were clearly a health threat. Why, only last year several people were hospitalized with salmonella poisoning that could have resulted from consuming contaminated eggs. It was incumbent on EGGS INCORPORATED to have this health threat removed. A salmonella poisoning epidemic, blamed on contaminated eggs, could be devastating to the EGGS INCORPORATED market. The board ordered the CEO to contact the EGGS INCORPORATED Lobbyist about the problem.

EGGS, inc. BOARD OF DIRECTORS MEET

AGENDA

- ### DESTRUCTIVE COMPETITION FROM INDEPENDENT EGG PRODUCERS

- ### POSSIBILITY OF CONTAMINATED EGGS AFFECTING MARKET DEMAND

- ### A SOLUTION TO BOTH PROBLEMS?

For years, the Lobbyist had protected the company from legislative and regulatory excesses. Now the Lobbyist must get more aggressive.

The Lobbyist met with several Legislators to explain the concern about the probability of contaminated eggs causing an epidemic and the destructive effect of the unfair competition from unregulated farmers, on EGGS INCORPORATED a large employer in their District. EGGS INCORPORATED had been a longtime supporter of all the Legislators contacted by the Lobbyist. Of course, the Legislators sympathized with the Lobbyist and wanted to help their supporter but were concerned about a reaction from farmers and the people who felt that the "free range" eggs were more nutritious than the eggs produced by EGGS INCORPORATED's caged chickens. Just look at the trouble the ingrates had made over raw milk. It would be both better and faster to use the Bureaucracy to achieve the desired results and the Legislators would escape any blame. The Legislators arranged a meeting between the Lobbyist and the Bureaucracy. The Legislators would request cooperation in the matter from the Bureaucrats.

Meeting with the Bureaucrat, the Lobbyist explains the threat of an epidemic from contaminated eggs and destructive competition to EGGS INCORPORATED by unregulated farmers who could possibly market contaminated eggs. The Bureaucrat was an expert in the desecration of the free market and possessed guile that any "con" man would envy. The Bureaucrat knew that it was best to implement new regulations in the smallest increments practical and affecting as few people as possible with each advancing increment. Exploiting his knowledge of the system, the Bureaucrat formulates a plan to solve EGG INCOPORATED's problems and presents it to the Lobbyist. The Bureaucrat was elated; new regulations would justify an increase in the Bureaucracy's budget, the Holy Grail of the Bureaucracy. Perhaps, even the creation of a new department with the Bureaucrat as the department head. He would be the Director of Eggs.

EGGS INCORPORATED LOBBYIST VISITS THE LEGISLATOR

LOBBYIST

LEGISLATOR &
CONSTITUENT

LOBBYIST EXPLAINS THE PROBLEM TO THE LEGISLATOR

- CONTAMINATED EGGS COULD CAUSE A SERIOUS EPIDEMIC. HIS CONSTITUENTS MUST BE PROTECTED.

- DANGEROUS & UNREGULATED FARMERS ARE ADVERSELY AFFECTING HIS SUPPORTERS' MARKET.

The plan was to create a regulation eliminating the "free range" eggs first. Fewer people were involved in the production of eggs using "free range" chickens and there should be little problem implementing such a regulation and removing the dangerous product from the market. Public hearings would be required, but those hearings would only be publicized and held in Washington DC. Of course there are no "free range" chickens in that city, so only Bureaucrats and EGGS INCORPORATED, testifying for the new regulations, would attend the hearings. There would be no one to object to the new regulations. The victims of the new anti "free range" egg regulations would not even find out about the new regulations until they were cited for the violations. Since the bureaucracy operates on a "guilty until proven innocent" basis, the sanctions would be applied immediately. Fighting the regulations and citations in court would require an expensive and extended legal action that the "mom and pop" farms could never afford.

Once the dust is settled from the anti "free range" egg regulations, the operation will be repeated to eliminate the remaining competition, mostly "mom and pop" operations that generally sold their product to friends and neighbors.

The new regulations to eliminate the possibility of contaminated eggs would require expensive equipment and costly inspections. The specified equipment was already in use in EGG INCOPORATED's factories. To prevent production of contaminated eggs, inspections of egg producing facilities would be mandatory. These costly inspections (fees to be determined on a per inspection basis, not per egg basis) would ensure the quality of the eggs available to the general public. The inspections alone would make the cost of producing small quantities of eggs uneconomical. The unfair competition to EGGS INCORPORATED would be eliminated.

The plan was implemented and the anti "free range" eggs regulations were imposed. Notice of the new rule was published in all the newspapers in State Capitols.
The government inspector learned that the proud, prosperous farmer had "free range" chickens and cited the farmer for violating the "new anti "free range chicken rule." The citation:

1. Imposed a fine for violating the "anti-free range" chicken rule. Marketing eggs from free range chickens was not allowed.
2. All eggs from the free range chickens would be recalled at the farmer's expense.
3. Chickens would be immediately caged and quarantined for two weeks to purge the chickens of the contaminated food.
4. Eggs from the chickens could not be marketed until the quarantine ended.
5. The facility would be inspected to ensure that all the dangerous practices had been terminated before marketing the eggs could be resumed.

FARMER CITED FOR MARKETING EGGS FROM FREE RANGE CHICKENS

BUREAUCRAT

FARMER

SANCTIONS APPLIED TO FARMER

1. FINE
2. RECALL EGGS
3. MUST CAGE CHICKENS
4. MARKETING OF EGGS PROHIBITED FOR 2 WEEKS TO DECONTAMINATE CHICKENS
5. FACILITIES TO BE INSPECTED BEFORE MARKETING THE EGGS COULD RESUME

BUREAUCRAT PROMISES THAT THE PUBLIC WILL BE PROTECTED FROM CONTAMINATED EGGS

Commonsense21c.com

BUREAUCRAT ORDERS FARMER'S CHICKENS CAGED

POOR CHICKENS DON'T UNDERSTAND THEIR MISFORTUNE. WHAT DID THEY DO TO DESERVE THIS?

Commonsense21c.com

The farmer had to borrow the money to buy approved cages. The cost of destroying all those "dangerous" eggs and the investment in cages wiped out over a year's earnings. Egg production was down for 6 weeks and the farmer's eggs no longer commanded the premium price of the "free range" eggs. The farmer was thrown deeply into debt and in danger of losing his farm.

In 15 years of producing eggs from "free range" chickens there had never been a problem so the farmer was at a loss to understand why the new regulations were implemented. However, the cost of challenging the Bureaucracy in court exceeded the value of his farm. His whole business plan was in jeopardy. This was the first time in his 15 years of operating the farm that he would lose money. If he could just hold on until the new crop came in, perhaps cash flow from the new corn crop and eggs sales would allow him to change his business plan and save the farm. After all, the farm had been in his family for years.

Just when the farmer thought that it could not get any worse, the Bureaucracy implemented new regulations requiring all egg producers to use equipment conforming to the Bureaucracy's specifications. Periodic inspections would be required and only producers that passed the inspection would be allowed to market eggs. The Bureaucracy would impose huge fines for marketing eggs from facilities that had not passed inspection. Of course, a short "grace" period was allowed to allow the egg producers to conform to the new regulations.

BUREAUCRAT IMPLEMENTS SECOND STAGE OF PLAN

NEW RULES FOR EGG PRODUCERS, REQUIRED TO PREVENT THE EPIDEMICS CAUSED BY CONTAMINATED EGGS

1. EQUIPMENT USED FOR THE CARE & FEEDING OF EGG PRODUCING CHICKENS MUST BE APPROVE BY THE "DEPARTMENT OF EGG PRODUCTION."
2. NEW EQUIPMENT MUST BE APPROVED BY THE "DEPARTMENT OF EGG PRODUCTION" BEFORE EGGS CAN BE MARKETED.
3. EGG PRODUCERS MUST BE INSPECTED AT INTERVALS SPECIFIED BY THE "DEPARTMENT OF EGG PRODUCTION."
4. EGG PRODUCERS WILL BE RESPONSIBLE FOR THE COST OF THE INSPECTION.

Commonsense21c.com

Because of the debt and the losses caused by the earlier regulations, the farmer was unable to obtain a loan to upgrade his operation to conform to the new regulations and loss of the income from egg sales would prevent him from servicing the debt that had already been incurred. Even if capital had been available, the farmer would have been unable to produce eggs at a competitive price. His operation was just too small to afford the inspection fees. Unable to service the debt and pay the taxes, the farm went into foreclosure and was sold at auction. The once proud, prosperous and productive farmer was reduced to a minimum wage job, existing in poverty with little hope of regaining his prosperity.

This poor farmer was just one of many to be done in by these regulations and the consumer soon saw the results in egg prices. Many of the farmers complained to their Legislators but all were told that the new regulations were created by the Bureaucracy and there was little Congress could do but they would certainly look into the problem and try to reign in the "out of control" Bureaucracy.

The new Bureaucratic regulation reduced egg production causing the price of eggs to increase. Naturally, EGGS INCORPORATED's profit increased and the Board of Directors looked forward to a bright future. The company held a huge party for all employees and bonuses were paid to the CEO, members of the Board and the Lobbyist.

WINNERS & LOSERS

WINNER: EGGS INCORPORATED

1. COMPETITION ELIMINATED
2. INCREASED PROFITS

LOSER: FARMER & FAMILY

LOSES HOME, FARM, PROFITABLE BUSINESS DESTROYED AND FORCED INTO MINIMUM WAGE JOB LIVING IN THE SLUMS

LOSER: THE CONSUMER (YOU)

1. INCREASE IN PRICE OF EGGS
2. "FREE RANGE CHICKEN" EGGS NOT AVAILABLE
3. YOU COULD BE THE NEXT VICTIM OF THE BUREAUCRAT!

The incident proved again that the printing of money was not the only cause of inflation. EGGS INCORPORATED prospered and the hapless consumer had no idea why egg prices increased.
The Board of Directors and the CEO recognized that the good fortune was the result of political power and not productivity. The budget of the Lobbyist was increased significantly and campaign contributions to their Legislator friends were enhanced. Members of the Board of Directors and the CEO held fund raisers for the friendly politicians.

EGGS INCORPORATED had found that in a mixed economy, political power was ever so much more important than productivity or even the consumer's preference.

The Bureaucracy had the power to enhance their prosperity or destroy the company. Both the Board of Directors and the CEO knew it. EGGS INCORPORATED settled into a period of prosperity, secure in the knowledge that their political power protected them from any competitor.

What could possibly hurt them now?

INVENTION CONVERTS CORN DIRECTLY TO EGGS NO CHICKENS REQUIRED

REDUCES COST OF EGGS BY 75%

CHOICE OF FLAVORS
STEAK
STRAWBERRY
CHOCOLATE
CRANBERRY
OYSTER
SHRIMP
EVEN EGG

OTHER ADVANTAGES
AMBIENT TEMPERATURE STORAGE
NON-ALLERGENIC
LONG SHELF LIFE
MAYBE MOLDED INTO APPETIZING SHAPES
REPLACES EGGS IN ALL RECIPES
WORLD HUNGER PROBLEM SOLVED

CAN EGGS INCORPORATED SURVIVE THIS?

Commonsense21c.com

Of course, technology can always be a problem to an established industry and tragedy struck! An inventor developed a device that could produce eggs directly from corn. The cost of eggs produced by the device was estimated to be 75% less than of the cost of a chicken produced egg.

Not only does the egg cost considerably less but it can be produced in a variety of flavors. Strawberry, chocolate, oysters and even egg are just some of the flavors available. If the device advances from the prototype stage to production, EGGS INCORPORATED will be decimated. All of their production facilities will be obsolete. The company would be unable to compete with the egg machine, either in price or quality. Thousands of their employees would lose their jobs.

The Board of Directors OF EGGS INCOPORATED met in a panic. How could they possibly compete with such a device? Somehow, they had to stop this madman from destroying their market. Again, they called upon their Lobbyist for help. It was a long shot but the Lobbyist was their only hope. To make a long story short, the Lobbyist and his Bureaucrat buddies found that the device emitted carbon dioxide. The "Great Global Warming Scam" came to the rescue. The Bureaucrats outlawed the device because of carbon dioxide emissions and excessive energy use. EGGS INCORPORATED was saved again by their Lobbyist and Bureaucrats.

"GREAT GLOBAL WARM SCAM"
SAVES EGGS INCORPORATED!

BUREAUCRAT

THE BUREAUCRAT SPEAKS:

NO!! NOT IN 21 CENTURY AMERICA!
THE EXTRAVAGANT USE OF ENERGY &
CARBON DIOXIDE EMISSIONS
WILL NOT BE TOLERATED!

THE BUREAUCRACY'S MISSION IS TO
EXPAND THEIR BUDGET & ENRICH
THE ARISTOCRACY

WORLD HUNGER IS NOT THE
BUREAUCRACY'S PROBLEM

Commonsense21c.com

The "technology dividend" took another hit from the Bureaucracy. The bureaucratic rules and regulations saved EGGS INCORPORATED but destroyed a device that could have helped to alleviate world hunger. How many times in the past 50 years has Bureaucratic, meddling in the free market destroyed an invention with the capacity to increase our standard of living. The Bureaucracy's purpose is to maintain the "Status Quo" and enhance the fortunes of the Aristocracy.

This fable is a fictional account of how the bureaucracy works and the havoc, it can, and has caused to our economy. Much of inflation is caused by the use of Bureaucratic force to artificially increase the cost of almost everything we buy. The covertly outlawing an invention that could enhance our productivity is the normal operation of the Bureaucracy. It has a devastating effect on real economic growth.

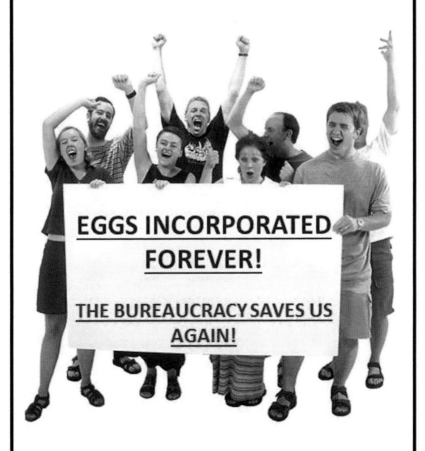

The villain of this fable is not the company, EGGS INCORPORATED; the villain is the Legislators and their puppet, the Bureaucracy that initiates the use of force against the individual. When the government substitutes force for the action of the free market, everyone loses in the long run!

This article may not be all fiction. When was the last time you saw an "EGGS FOR SALE" sign on a farmer's lawn?

EPILOGUE

Ayn Rand once stated that she wrote about **"life as it could be, and should be."** "A Toby's Fable is about **"life as it is and should not be."** This is a fictional tale and the reader should not take the Bureaucratic procedures literally.

The Bureaucracy is the Aristocracy's weapon of choice! Did you ever wonder why the Bureaucracy is so effective in the Aristocracy's battle against the Patriot? The Bureaucracy creates new rules daily and when the Bureaucracy makes the determination that you have violated those rules you are guilty until proven innocent in a court of law.

The Bureaucracy's ruling stands until it is overturned by the Courts. Few people have the resources to challenge the Bureaucracy in court and even fewer are willing to squander their fortune and effort on a fool's errand. By the time the Court acts, the results will, most likely, be irrelevant, the damage to the victim beyond repair. So in most cases the Bureaucracy's ruling stands without challenge.

The cartoon, "6 Powers of the Bureaucracy" shows how the Bureaucracy trumps your Constitutional rights.

The cartoon "You V/S the Bureaucracy" illustrates the futility of challenging the Bureaucracy.

BIRTH OF THE BUREAUCRACY

What conditions led to the creation of the Bureaucracy? See the following Cartoon, "Birth of the Bureaucracy.

BIRTH OF THE BUREAUCRACY-1888

RAILROADS & THE GRANGE (A LARGE FARMERS ORGANIZATION) SEEK FAVORABLE FREIGHT RATES BY APPLYING PRESSURE TO THE CONGRESS

THE GRANGE   THE RAILROADS
LOW RATES   HIGH RATES

ATTEMPTING TO EVADE RESPONSIBILITY, CONGRESS CREATES THE INTERSTATE COMMERCE COMMISSION (ICC) THE BUREAUCRACY IS BORN!

THE BUREAUCRACY HAS EVOLVED INTO THE PRIMARY TOOL USED BY POLITICIANS TO REWARD THEIR CRONIES AND PUNISH POLITICAL DISSENT!

Commonsense21c.com

CAN A BLOODY REVOLUTION BE AVOIDED?

The greatest danger to the Republic is the Aristocracy's use of the Bureaucracy to punish political dissent.

A Republic cannot survive when the Aristocracy uses government force (IRS, EPA and Justice Department) to suppress political dissent!

Where is the outrage? Mr. Obama has committed numerous "high crimes and misdemeanors." Many of these infractions use government force to discourage and suppress political dissent

It took an Independent Special Prosecutor to bring down Richard Nixon. Of course, Mr. Obama knows this. Will that Congress create an Independent Special Prosecutor, or will the eunuchs in Congress protect their patron and allow the Republic to be destroyed.

The appointment of an Independent Special Prosecutor is our last chance to avoid a bloody revolution most likely ending in a dictatorship!

Those who collaborate with the Aristocracy will receive their rewards. Just as Hitler's collaborators received their reward during the "Night of the Long Knives."

See the cartoon, "Can a Bloody Revolution, Ending in a Dictatorship be Avoided?"

CAN A BLOODY REVOLUTION
ENDING IN A DICTATORSHIP BE AVOIDED?

A SPECIAL INDEPENDENT PROSECUTOR IS OUR LAST CHANCE!

INDEPENDENT PROSECUTOR WITH THE POWER TO

1. IDENTIFY & HALT THE OPPRESSION OF POLITICAL DISSENT BY THE BUREAUCRACY & JUSTICE DEPARTMENT

2. PROSECUTE THOSE RESPONSIBLE FOR THE OPPRESSION

OR REPEAT

LEXINGTON GREEN

" THE SHOT HEARD 'ROUND THE WORLD"

Commonsense21c.com

POLITICAL DISSENT:
THE LIFE BLOOD OF THE REPUBLIC

Commonsense21c.com

CAPITALISM–THE FIRST 100 YEARS

The implementation of the United States Constitution, led to over 100 years of prosperity and technological development that is unrivaled in history.

See the cartoon, "Capitalism Performance" to see some of the achievements made possible by the freedom and liberty protected by the Constitution before it was corrupted by the Aristocracy.

CAPITALISM PERFORMANCE

CHEAP & ABUNDANT ENERGY
STANDARD OIL inc. REDUCED THE
COST OF KEROSENE FROM
$0.58 /GAL IN 1865
TO $0.074 /GAL IN 1890.

REDUCED THE PORTION OF
THE POPULATION REQUIRED
TO PRODUCE FOOD FROM 41%
TO LESS THAN 1.9%

ALCOA CREATED THE ALUMINUM
INDUSTRY WITH ALL THE PROSPERITY
& INNOVATION CREATED BY THAT
LIGHT, STRONG METAL.

THOMAS EDISON PRODUCES
THE LIGHT BULB AND CREATES
THE ELECTRICAL UTILITY
INDUSTRY.

OBJECTIVE OF THE ENTREPRENEUR IS THE CREATION OF WEALTH

Commonsense21c.com

THE END

BOOKS BY FELTON (TOBY) WILLIAMSON, Jr.

"21st CENTURY COMMON SENSE"
Explains how we have allowed the Aristocracy to destroy our flawed capitalistic system and replace it with the tyranny of King George III, under new management. The disastrous results of the Aristocracy's five highly touted programs:
- The Income Tax Laws
- Inflation
- Antitrust Laws
- Earmarks
- The Bureaucracy

Included in the book are the economic advantages of the "Technology Dividend", the greatest threat to our Republic, and a recipe to regain our freedom and prosperity are included.

"COMMON SENSE THE WAY BACK"
An abridged version of "21st CENTURY COMMON SENSE"

"THE TEA PARTY & THE TYRANT"
A group of articles describing the conflict between the Tea Party and the Aristocracy

"CARTOONS OF COERCION"
A collection of 40 outrageous cartoons. If a picture is worth 1000 words, the 40 cartoons in "Cartoons of Coercion" contain a lot of material for a book with only 5,000 words of text. This is not a book you read; you just enjoy the pictures.

Short sections of text explain the purpose of and conditions that led to the creation of these cartoons.

Each of the illustrations is listed in the Table of Contents and may be accessed by clicking on the title of the illustration. The purpose of this format is to allow the reader to easily use the Kindle, iPod or other device to show specific cartoons to a friend.

The reader is cautioned to be very selective in displaying these cartoons to the Public. Showing these cartoons to the Aristocracy or those who support the Aristocracy may provoke hostility or inflame an existing medical emergency condition.

May you enjoy these cartoons as much as the Author enjoyed preparing them.

"TEA PARTY AND THE TYRANT – LIBERTY V/S TYRANNY" "21st CENTURY COMMON SENSE" "COMMON SENSE – THE WAY BACK"

Commonsense21c.com contains information on all these books. These books are available at Amazon.com and most book stores.
All these books are available in the Kindle Edition.

"A TOBY'S FABLE"

"A Toby's Fable" is a fictional account of the Aristocracy, using the Bureaucracy to increase the profits of their cronies. The action drives small farmers out of business and limits consumer's choices. While the specifics of this story, a fictional, similar oppression is all too common in our society. Are you at risk? .

"A Toby's fable" is more like a long, fully illustrated magazine article than a book. But you won't find a better description of the creeping tyranny that is destroying America.

The book contains 19 illustrations in full color.

Proof

Made in the USA
Charleston, SC
23 February 2014